MW01248299

Find Your Soul
In Your Heart

Wisdom Teachings & Heart Centred Meditations

HILARY BOWRING

ISBN: 979-8-89031-658-5 (sc)
ISBN: 979-8-89031-659-2 (hc)
ISBN: 979-8-89031-660-8 (e)

THE EWINGS
PUBLISHING

One Galleria Blvd., Suite 1900, Metairie, LA 70001
(504) 702-6708

PRAISE FOR
Find Your Soul

"**Thank you for sharing your wisdom.** You have touched my heart with the honesty and purity of your heart! In *Find Your Soul* the simple truth shines through, realizing we have the power and the choice to change and grow through each experience; also provides us with practical and divine tools to reach that space of tranquility and joy, setting us free from the burdens of the ego."
Fran Hall. Communications volunteer

"**A pleasure to read and full of nuggets of wisdom.**" Truly an inspiring read, to resonate with her words, teachings, and meditations." Hilary's book has inspired me to set aside 5 minutes a day to meditate -what a pleasure to choose from nine different meditations.
Nicole Piller. Pilates & Yoga Teacher

"**Let's Play and Say YES to Life.** This book is written with loving guidance which shows us how to enjoy unlimited possibilities. Hilary reveals her soul in her writing and this encourages the reader to practice her meditations, connect with inner peace and say YES to life."
Lois Ferguson. Nutritionist

"**An excellent book for both people who are experienced and those new to self discovery and meditation**, succinct, informative and warmly written. It introduced me to new ways of looking at everyday situations with appropriate powerful meditations. She relates her work to personal experiences as well as worldwide situations. I can confidently recommend it!"
Brenda Spence. Teacher.

"**Loved this book!,** beautifully written with a hopeful belief that we can all evolve to a kinder place, by linking to our soul to our hearts. I particularly appreciated the bite size meditation lessons. I know I will re-visit these pages often as I explore meditation and connect with my soul's desires."
Janet Whitney. Entrepreneur

"**An essential tool that speaks directly to our evolutionary shift as humanity** and supports soul journeying. Hilary's resourceful intelligence and humble spirit met me at the seat of my soul. I saw the 'other one of me' that is on a light-working journey. To meet the creator within!"
Biljana. Shamanic artist.

Mindful of imminent spiritual change I highly recommend this thought provoking book that takes the mystery out of meditation. It is well thought out and well written, short and concise and is coming straight from her heart."
Tim Shaw. Retired Pharmacist

Filled with her wisdom and many wonderful and effective methods to help us on our own meditative journey.
Margaret Jackson. Retired Teacher

INTRODUCTION

E very major religion predicted that the beginning of the 21st century would be one of radical change. Some prophesies include frightening earth changes: earthquakes, typhoons, etc., with a lot of destruction and devastation. However, many modern spiritual thinkers see the earth crisis as the culmination of humanity's collective spiritual upheaval, the physical symbols of the conflict between our selfish ego needs and the soul's desire to connect with our universal source. If we follow our soul, it is possible to ward off Armageddon and gently transition into a new era of unity consciousness.

This new era is a global shift in human consciousness where we become more heart centered and understand that we are part of one consciousness, and unlock our natural compassion and care for one another. For the new world to unfold, old structures will need to break apart, especially our financial systems where wealth sits in the hands of a few, which is counter to the opportunity to end poverty and treat everyone with love and respect. We don't know what our new world will look like, as it's hard to envision something outside of our current awareness. It is best not to resist the changes through fear of the unknown, but to flow with what feels right intuitively for each of us. If we follow our heart's intelligence on a daily basis, something new and magical will be created.

When we evolve to full heart-consciousness, we collectively care for the welfare of everyone. If we think of our lives as being of service, we become enthusiastic and creative; we collaborate and co-create with one another. We shift away from being subject to the will of authoritarian governments, leaders and hierarchical systems and recognize our collective power to create. We have the spiritual maturity to wisely handle the power of what we have created, and what we can create in the future.

In the transition, life is acutely hectic, stressful and forever changing, inspiring us to be more flexible and mobile with our responses to ongoing challenges. There is no longer the stability of the same steady job, the same mom and dad; no more days of pastoral peace following the rhythm of nature and the flow of the seasons. Although there is a revival of thought that we would be better served if we turned our attention toward nature again: renew our respect for beautiful planet earth by showing regard for her rhythm of life and death and accept that death brings the opening for new cycles to begin - perennial teachings!

Another way to move through the transition is to become more soulful. The soul is like a flame in our hearts, our guiding light and connection to our Source. Our ego has forgotten this light and became preoccupied with the physical body, the physical world; trapped by desires and attachments to material things. Conversely, following the wisdom of our soul and nurturing ourselves from within, strengthens us and brings freedom from external influences, because we are able to access our internal source of fearlessness, such that we remain steady no matter what happens on the outside.

An evolutionary shift is happening whether we like it or not. It's an unstoppable force. Our choices on how we live our daily lives will affect the outcome of this change. Tuning into our soul for guidance will bring forth better choices. If we make a commitment to manifest our highest potential and help others to do the same, I'm very hopeful that everything will turn out better than we could possibly imagine.

This book is about finding your soul, as the soul is our connection to the bigger picture holding the wisdom to align us with the evolutionary shift in consciousness. We connect with our soul in the heart, the seat of the soul, most powerfully in meditation. The book gives many heart centred meditations from ancient tantric scriptures that deepen our ability to discern soul guidance from ego-driven directions, to manifest our greatest potential. There are also exercises to help open our hearts to live a more soulful existence and methods to quantum leap into a new version of ourselves!

I hope you try the meditations! Meditation builds our inner strength so we can be stable and serene no matter what life serves in these extreme times. There is also the potential gift of experiencing our divine nature and a state of bliss when we maintain our commitment to meditate.

My life has been dedicated to following my soul guidance since my husband David's sudden death. My search for the meaning of life intensified to say the least! After an extremely prolonged period of grief, lasting several years, I gradually unveiled a new way of looking at things. I began to see life and its challenges as a soul's journey to expand awareness of the human condition and deepen our compassion for one another - to realize we are spirits in a human body, and that existence continues in the subtle realms. This appreciation can expand our ability to endure pressure, because we truly understand that we are more than a physical body. We are eternal Spirit. During the years of grief and soul searching, I followed daily soul guidance and evolved from being an advertising executive to a spiritual counsellor and meditation teacher - 'jobs' that never existed in my imagination. The jobs 'became', as I 'unfolded'.

It is said that if just 10 percent of humanity is prepared to change - to shift understanding that our true nature is divine, that we are part of one consciousness, affecting each other, it will be enough to help all of humanity shift. To make the quantum leap outside the paradigm of suffering, to a world full of grace with plenty of abundance for everyone.

Through my own commitment to a daily meditation practice, even for five minutes, makes a difference. I am a radiant, healthy human being with an inner strength that supports me through challenges. I want to smile at everyone and feel them smile back - even in the darkest moments to feel love and be able to say I love you. If anyone, after reading this book, is willing to put forth the effort to meditate and self-change, and become one of the 10 percent, our souls would be very pleased indeed!

CONTENTS

CHAPTER 1

We Each have a Role to Play in the Evolutionary Shift

A time of wonder and awe

Here we are, incarnated at the beginning of the 21st century. There is no mistake why we are here now. We are destined to be involved in an evolutionary shift in human consciousness - a time of wonder and awe. It is an incredible time of awakening and powerful energetic shifts of extraordinary spiritual transformation - where we recognize our divinity, creative power and interconnection.

> *"Humanity is going to experience a breakthrough-a new life; a new civilization; a new body-mind."* Sri Siva

It is said, if we envision a truly magnificent, abundant and joyful life for humanity, we can experience miracles now. Now is the time to live our soul purpose with unlimited possibilities, rather than the limited ego-governed life we have been living.

Soul Blueprints and Destinies

Our soul blueprint was seeded at birth with the unique role we are each to play in assisting this spiritual breakthrough. We are empowered as a collective to bring about change and each has a role, no matter how seemingly small. Each one of us matters. Without our individual contribution, there's a lessening of the impetus to change. We all need to generate enough energy to make a quantum leap forward to boost humanity's advancement.

There's no *pressure* to find the role we are each to play. It's allowing it to unfold on a daily basis to a destiny of our highest potential.

A shift from 'I' to 'We' Consciousness

The evolution is accelerating. There are teachers abound now-a-days who are generously sharing their thoughts and ideas freely on the internet, trying to help humankind make the shift. For instance, there are those who teach how to perfect manifestation to create a better material life, and others teach techniques on how to clear emotional blocks around past hurts, which is great. Leading evolutionary teachers sense a radical shift is needed to move us from the ego-governance of our lives a dropping of the personal 'I', to 'We' consciousness. We are now ready enough, healed enough to move forward in an inter-connected way. We needed to have had enough 'Me' consciousness in order to be clear about who we are individually first in order to unconditionally help others.

The spiritual goal for each of us is to fulfill our greatest soul potential for our collective advancement.

As part of 'We' consciousness, we need to envisage helping humanity evolve as an under-pinning to our personal growth, because when we grow, everyone grows. It's not just about us. It's about everyone and being aware of this intensifies the effect. Even simple things such as: if I forgive someone, everyone is positively affected; if I make someone laugh, everyone feels the energy; if I meditate, everyone benefits.

This shift is a radical change in outlook, where any selfish motives are assuaged by desires for the collective wellbeing. We are transitioning to a time in which our soul purpose overrides the issues of our limited ego self; a time to be aware of impulses to be active, be creative, be in service to humanity, with full respect for one's self and others. A delicate balance is needed.

Understanding our One-ness

Eastern philosophy understands our One-ness in tandem with our diversity. The philosophy I draw on is a high vibrational stream of tantric scriptures where the essential teaching is, there is One Consciousness which pulsates in a diversity of forms. The unique you and the unique me are still part of the same One, the same energy. These teachings give the biggest picture possible to raise our consciousness, describing life as a play of consciousness: from concealment to revelation. Concealment of our divinity to then experience the joyous revelation that we are in fact divine. It's like a play in which each one of us play different parts for our evolutionary growth from concealment to revelation, like the game of hide and seek. But things went a bit wrong when our ego began to believe we are only the physical body, only a personality that feels separate and alone. A veil of forgetfulness of our true nature cloaked us. Over many life times our mistaken sense of identity by the ego filled us with aloneness and created more separation - a strong sense of 'them' and 'us' developed even demonizing certain peoples and groups. An ever deepening isolation ensued. The first step to liberation is to accept that we are all part of One Consciousness, even if it's only intellectually at first, then with consistent spiritual practices the experience of One-ness and self-realization occurs. It is not easy to believe that we are "One" as the play of consciousness is set up with polarities, the pairs of opposites, you/me, hot/cold, love/hate, etc., and we get drawn into them. The differences are part of the experience in the play; we cannot know the light without the contrast of the dark. Seeing our similarities is hard too and requires contemplation. Love is the core value we all share. It is love that dissolves our differences!

A second step to liberation is to see how dualistic thinking pervades our life, and governs our reactions to situations. Wisdom comes when we can step outside this paradigm and see our One-ness, and when problems arise, respond with solutions to benefit everyone's highest good. Grace flows when our intention is to benefit others. **The following meditation helps us connect with our One-ness.**

One-ness Meditation

Sit quietly where you can relax without any disturbance. Close your eyes and place your hands on your lap. If sitting in a chair, place your feet hip-width apart, firmly planted on the ground and feel roots from the soles of your feet going down into the earth. If sitting cross legged feel the roots extending down from your sitting bones…

Relax your shoulders and gently elongate your spine. Feel your connection with the divine realms above through the crown chakra at the top of your head. You are now in alignment with the earth below and heaven above. Focus on your heart and place your hands in prayer position, and watch the flow of your breath…Take a couple of deep breaths in…and deep breaths out to release any tension…

Silently ask for the Light of Consciousness to come to you - the Light that includes Universal Love and Grace - the source of our divinity and wisdom individually and collectively. Ask to be connected with our One-ness, as well as our diversity…

Focus on the flow of your breath in and out of your heart. Think of it as being a universal breath that flows through each person that draws us together. With each breath honour the universal breath…

Allow yourself time to feel and hear the rhythm of your breath as it goes in and out…

Become aware of the presence of the universal light all around you, enveloping you, embracing you. The Light is filled with love, wisdom and grace. Feel your interconnection with everything and everyone. Feel One-ness…

Breathe in this loving energy, breathe out thanks. In giving and receiving, you no longer feel alone. Allow yourself to settle into the awareness of your One-ness with this Light…

Breathe in the feeling of One-ness and breathe out, gratitude and allow yourself to stay in this state for a few minutes.

Video version on YouTube:
https://youtu.be/Y1ZTvZkf66c?si=VChjEV0TZClMRMbZ

Meditation Insight(s) / Reflection

Use this page to write what came up for you in your *One-ness Meditation.* If nothing at all arose, don't worry, insights often occur some time after meditation.

Worldly and Spiritual Fulfilment

The evolutionary shift is not about ignoring our physical life. Tantric spiritual practices are to help us experience divinity and bliss in our bodies. Tantra is a diverse range of ancient Indian oral traditions, outlining practical systems of spiritual practices for a good physical and spiritual life. 'Tantra' means book, theory (revealed by God). The root 'Tan' means expansion, 'tra' means save, protect (from the cycle of suffering). The aim is to expand our awareness and our capacity for joy, with love and respect for each other. Tantric practices are designed to help us experience our true nature as divine in this body, in this lifetime and consciously enjoy the physical world of pleasures and wealth in the context of understanding our spiritual essence and our One-ness.

Tantra, revolutionary in its time, is a path of embodiment for 'everyman' to experience their personal divinity. While the traditions of Yoga and Hinduism teach that the only way to experience God directly is to transcend the body, the senses and our desires. Those who were bestowed the awareness of our divine nature were ascetics and Brahmin priests. So too in Christianity, priests and nuns were the only ones connected with God through austere practices and celibacy. Tantra revealed that everyone is divine and able to experience God in everyday life, be regular householders with normal lives and that the body too is divine. Rather than transcend our bodies and senses, we can experience bliss in the body. We don't have to go to heaven and disembody to feel 'the love beyond our understanding'. Tantric sages knew how to: open gateways to experience divinity in the body; teach the physical body to experience the subtle body and how to sense the subtle energy. **Tantra is about knowing the subtle body** - to bring body, mind, heart and spirit together.

The Tantric attitude is, *"The divine is in everything"*. The seeds of enlightenment are within **every experience**, not a hierarchy of when I'm a better person, I'll get enlightened! The potential to know our divinity is in every experience, every humble daily pastime and in every challenge. Tantra teaches, *"Say yes to everything"*!

CHAPTER 2

Revealing our Soul Purpose

We each have a soul blueprint, seeded at birth like a plan for our potential soul purpose. There is no pressure to find out what this is. It's not like, "What is my role" in terms of a job. It's about revealing who we are in all our multiple facets; for example, our passions - what lights us up? - and following our dharma. The idea of dharma comes from Eastern philosophy. It means honouring and revealing our unique offerings. No one is exactly like another and each of us has a responsibility to express our distinctive self. Everything has a dharma to be itself, like a tree is to be a tree; that is its purpose.

Our purpose is to be our authentic divine selves

Our soul purpose is to be our authentic self, aligning with our soul's blueprint, rather than aligning with any personas developed by the small ego's mistaken sense of identity. Aligning with the ego, leads to conformance with what society wants us to be, what our family wants us to be, what our friends wants us to be. Wanting to be accepted can be the ego's way of overcoming the feeling of separation. 'If I fit in, I won't feel so alone'. Over many lifetimes, we have acted completely out of alignment with our soul's nature and become more and more emotionally detached and even ill. In this lifetime, the veils of separation are being dissolved. We have the opportunity to feel our real identity, to have the courage to be exactly who we are, including our shadow sides, and embrace our unique nature with foibles and all. When we move into acceptance of all these aspects, and can see the beauty of the rough inside the smooth, the devil inside the saint, we can laugh and engage with the play of consciousness! When we embrace our quirks and stop trying to be acceptable to others, we shift into I AM nature. At the same time, dharma has a moral code to be consciously human. We don't kill, rape, persecute or knowingly cause harm to anyone or anything. We take responsibility for our actions and when we inadvertently hurt others we say we are sorry, knowing all hurts wound everyone for we are "One" and the more alert we are to that, the more caring and loving we can become.

Be comfortable with the unknown and with our own power

We are being told we are more powerful than we think! Now we are ready 'enough' to fulfill our greatest soul potential in full alignment with our divine nature. But are we willing to let go of our deeply cherished beliefs and allow space for the unknown? Are we open to looking beyond what we already know? If we can expand our awareness, new doors are opened to higher wisdom and the fields of pure creative potential to find our soul purpose. It starts with becoming comfortable with the unknown and letting go of expectations; then moving to a mind-set where we can imagine a great creative power inside us. As we accept our divine nature, we become co-creators and can access that primal energy that created us!

The ego is very important for manifestation

The ego is our individual will power and our inborn ability to manifest whatever we desire consciously, and unconsciously. We most definitely need our ego - our will power to manifest anything. The shift we need to make is being aware of *who* is directing. The soul is meant to be in command, inspiring our ego and mind to manifest *its* desires. In the past, we simply forgot who was to lead, due to the disconnection with *all that is*. If we were to reverse the roles as they were originally, it will be fantastic. For when the ego moves into alignment with the soul, we connect with the bigger picture and move beyond our selfish desires and whims. When the ego is aligned with our soul, all is in synch like an arrow released perfectly from an archer's bow and the target is hit. Manifestation is rapid. To make this shift friendlier, we can laugh and have fun with our ego. Laughing at ourselves is a vital feature of the evolutionary shift!

Fun exercise: *Connecting with our soul through movement*
Put music on that you love...close your eyes and dance on the spot.
Turn your attention within and feel the inner energy guiding you to
express through your body. Be playful! That's your soul!

Discerning soul-guidance from 'small' ego influences

To be part of this huge transition requires distinguishing between soul-guidance and ego influence. We want to explore ways to clarify between these two different communication wavelengths. One clue is the ego is pretty serious, whereas the soul is playful. Soul ideas come spontaneously from inner wisdom, while the ego agonizes over solving problems. Ego is critical, the soul is unconditional, and furthermore, the soul loves your perfect imperfections, and loves your imperfect family and friends! The ego has responsibilities. The soul has passions! The soul is uncensored. It celebrates life, and says, "Yes" to everything: the good, the bad and the ugly, knowing it's all about expansion.

The ego is physical and the soul is subtle. We need to become more aware of our subtle body. Subtle energy reveals our soul purpose. One cornerstone practice, to expand this sensitivity, is meditation. Ask to have the energy of your soul revealed so you can resonate with ease and discern between soul-guidance and ego-ideas. **Here is a Tantric meditation technique to connect with our subtle body.**

Subtle Body Meditation

This meditation accesses the subtle body through the Third Eye.

Sit quietly where you can relax without any disturbance. Close your eyes and place your hands on your lap. If sitting in a chair, place your feet hip-width apart, firmly planted on the ground and feel roots from the soles of your feet going down into the earth. If sitting cross legged, feel the roots extending down from your sitting bones…

Relax your shoulders and gently elongate your spine. Take a couple of deep breaths in and deep breaths out to release any tension…

Focus your attention on the breath. Draw in the breath through your nostrils, with specific attention at the bottom of the nose between the two nostrils. As you gently breathe, notice how the in breath is cool and the out breath is warm. As you become more centred through placing your attention on the movement of the breath at the base of the nostrils, draw in the breath and direct it upwards to the hard palate at the roof of the mouth. Move the breath through the palate up to the centre of the skull, just behind the eye brows where the Third Eye chakra is located. Allow the inhalation to flow up and the exhalation to flow out through the forehead - through the space between the eyebrows. Focus on the breath moving up and feel the energy channel there. There is a path from the base of the nostril, through the hard palate to the Third Eye, which opens a doorway to the subtle body, the inward direction. Begin to feel a movement inwards…

If thoughts arise just let them be there. Don't get involved with them. Stay in this place where the mind becomes indrawn. Again, focus on the breath flowing in through the nostrils, through the centre of the skull behind the Third Eye and then flows out between the eyebrows. Breathing in and breathing out in this way, a steady state of calm fills you. You settle into the inward state of quietness. Ask to have the energy of your soul revealed, so you can resonate with ease and discern between soul-guidance and ego ideas.

A regular meditation practice will deepen the opening of the gateway and awareness of our soul-guidance; connect us with our intuition and with the evolutionary impulse of consciousness.

Meditation Insight(s) / Reflection

Use this page to write what came up for you in your *Subtle Body Meditation.* If nothing at all arose, insights often occur some time after meditation.

CHAPTER 3

Soul Journeys

The idea of soul journeys helps us to understand that life is an opportunity for spiritual learning and expansion - a journey to enlightenment. It takes a suspension of disbelief and openness to the idea of reincarnation. The premise is that we have had many lifetimes spent mainly in ignorance of our ability to create our lives with conscious and sub-conscious thoughts. We create karma: the consequences of our prevailing thoughts and actions. Some karma in this lifetime comes from thoughts and actions playing out from previous lifetimes. Without this perspective, we won't really understand why things happen to us: *"How come that negative thing happened to me when I've been a sweet saint all my life?"* Let alone why innocent children have very harsh life experiences.

In my case, my husband David died suddenly at age 44. I was completely devastated and in the place of, *why do bad things happen to good people.* That was back in 1994, when I had already opened to meditation and all sorts of spiritual thoughts. My husband was a recovering alcoholic, so we were both into spiritual ideas and I became a member of Al-Anon. I could really see the unfortunate truth that his difficulties and his slips helped me grow. I became stronger spiritually as he suffered. At his death, it was like my own. Everything I believed in was no longer valid and I had no sense of myself. I had believed that by living a good life, by being open to new ideas like meditation, and by learning spiritual ideas like detachment, would guarantee a great life. My husband even had a near death experience in hospital, a couple of years earlier, so we felt very confident that our lives would continue and get better. So his death flipped me out. It seemed so unfair, but it also expanded me beyond what would have been possible had he stayed alive. In the process, I had to zero-base my belief systems and be prepared to stay very open and vulnerable. It was like having no skin. In the end, it was too painful, so I put back on some of my old ego patterns, like an old coat for protection. After much grief, confusion and crying over my broken heart, along with a search to try to make sense of what had happened. I came across the idea of soul journeys.

In Michael Newton's book, *'Journey of Souls'*, he outlines that there is an agreement as souls in between lives to experience specific situations that would bring spiritual growth, and we do that with a group of soul mates who will play different roles in the dramas for the potential to expand all of us. There are no guarantees that we will each expand to our full potential, but that's the set up. As souls, we recognize that becoming enlightened means we understand we are divine. Over many lifetimes, we believed that we are separate and alone, and created many different ways to perpetuate this illusion. These beliefs and related thoughts became recurrent karmic patterns that governed lifetime after lifetime. Our 'karmic themes'. A group of soul mates with similar experiences can help each other gain wisdom and break the patterns.

Karmic Themes

Karmic themes are major life patterns that repeat and repeat. They are like a mosaic of the human condition of suffering. The most deeply-held wounds are: sexual abuse, abandonment, betrayal, persecution, martyrdom, suicide, and I guess murder is right up there. The other side of the coin, being the perpetrators of these violations is tragic too. Then there are other themes that run alongside the mega themes to further obscure our divinity: victimhood, caring what other people think, co-dependency, addiction, doing, doing, etc. Developing an awareness of all these patterns, and how they govern our lives, raise us to a new level of consciousness where we can make changes and new choices, and get on the path to freedom.

Recognizing Soul Journeys

The enlightenment that comes from simply recognizing the idea of soul journeys is huge. Our apparent enemies are soul friends and our most tragic moments are passages to growth. The heart knows our soul journey, as the heart is the seat of the soul. When we focus on our hearts, we are led back to soul wisdom and gain insights into the karmic themes in our life experience. We become open to evolve through them. If we recognize that life is a journey to expand our awareness, we will enjoy a more conscious way of living. **Try this meditation to gain insights.**

Meditation for Soul Connection and Insights about Your Soul Journey

Sit quietly where you can relax without any disturbance. Close your eyes and place your hands on your lap. If sitting in a chair, place your feet hip-width apart, firmly planted on the ground and feel roots from the soles of your feet going down into the earth. If sitting cross legged, feel the roots extending down from your sitting bones...

Relax your shoulders and gently elongate your spine. Take a couple of deep breaths in and deep breaths out to release any tension...

Focus your attention on your heart. Place your hands in prayer position and breathe into your hands your intention to enter the inner heart centre...

Breathe in to your heart; breathe out from your heart. Relax your hands and place them on your knees or lap. Breathe into your heart again and fill your whole body with breath. Then, exhale gently. Breathe deeply into your heart, as if reaching behind the physical heart to your back and connect with your inner heart centre. Breathe again into your back. Feel the vastness of the universal heart - of spacious awareness. Your front is about 'you', the individual, and your back is the connection to something greater than you: Universal Consciousness. Feel the vastness of the great heart, an expansive, limitless place...

Allow yourself to connect with that great heart: that inspiration, that intelligence, that creativity, that compassion and that joy, for you are *that*! Silently affirm, *"I AM Consciousness. I am open to understanding my soul journey, to identifying my karmic themes so I can evolve. I have the power to bring forth a new way of living, co-creating with others for peace, health and prosperity for all. I connect with the divine plan."*

Stay in silence now in this sacred place of the soul and wait for your soul to give you insights into your soul journey—it may be a visual or a feeling rather than words. And nothing may come forward at this very moment but insights may follow in the days ahead. Pause......and connect with your soul for a minute or two......2 min

Gently bring your attention back into the room and when you are ready open your eyes.

Video version on YouTube:
https://youtu.be/WCoWlMAwclQ?si=RrEUxZ64ReJkbEyn

Meditation Insight(s) / Reflection

Use this page to write what came up for you in your *Heart-Centred Meditation for Insights about Your Soul Journey*. If nothing at all arose don't worry as insights often occur some time after meditation.

CHAPTER 4

Opening our Hearts, the Seat of the Soul

Our hearts are closed, because of all the hurts we've endured. This closure cuts us off from any sense of our divinity and connection with our soul purpose. The heart is the centre of feeling of the most sensitive kind. Truly heartbreaking experiences do break our hearts and the pain is very physical. I know through personal experience in my grief when my heart felt two feet outside my body and hurting. The only relief was to cry, but that only appeased the pain until the next wave.

Face and feel the pain

We tend to protect our hearts from real feelings, and we have developed patterns that shield us from our own vulnerability and sensitivity. Our core hurts may be grief, betrayal, persecution – the conditions of the heart that Jesus bore to open us to love. Many times we use our mind to create distractions from the deep emotional pain of hurtful events, fearing the pain would be too great to bear. However, this pushes the unfelt pain into our bodies where it can come out as disease later on in life. If we can summon the courage to cry and sob, and release the painful feelings, our hearts expand and open. Eventually, we are able to offer more compassion to others and become more aware of the depths of our soul.

Letting go of negative emotions and fears

There is a direct path through the heart to connect with our divine nature. It is found at the *inner* heart centre - the seat of the soul and a very sacred place. Heart-centred meditation opens the gateway to this centre for us to *experience* our divinity and feel the energy of love, and a state of bliss in our bodies - a profound state we rarely, if ever feel! One of the ways we can start to open the gateway is by letting go of negative emotions and fears.

The heart centre carries positive and negative emotions. We can emanate upliftment or sorrow or fear from the heart field. Science has shown that the heart is the largest generator of electromagnetic energy in the body and the field extends up to 12 feet around each person. Our emotions not only drive us, but definitely affect others too. When we clear our own heart, we positively impact others; each one of us can make a difference.

The play of consciousness is constructed in polarities and a full range exists in our hearts. Positives include: love, hope, enthusiasm, courage, joy. Negatives are hate, despair, anxiety, fear, grief. We move through the range, depending on our life circumstance or experiences: from loyalty to betrayal, from hero to victim, from peace to anger. However, we can become stuck in the negative -once aware we can make a conscious choice to disconnect and move into neutrality. From there we can engage in more positive experiences that build the positive emotions for heart opening.

When we look at fear, there are multiple aspects of it. The current global economic conditions have many people dealing with survival fears: lack of financial resources, unemployment, and the stock market, for example. There are a lot of heavy hearts around the world, sending negative energies out, influencing all of us and feeding our fears. We can play our part in the Collective healing by **sending out positive emotions** of hope, trust, faith, etc., and we get there by releasing some of our own fears. I'm sure we have all felt some of the cultural fears, especially when the media is sensationalistic. We are like a battery, holding negative and positive charge in balance. We lose balance when we hold onto negative emotions. It builds up stress that adversely affects our physical and mental health. Letting go of deeply held resentments reduces stress hugely and we actually feel the relief!

One technique in meditation is to allow feelings to be *felt* (no more suppression) then release them to be dissolved into the vastness of the universal heart.

Letting Go of Fears into Universal Heart Meditation

Releases negative emotions and dissolves them in the universal heart...

Drop your shoulders and gently elongate your spine. Take a deep breath in and a deep breath out. It is time to relax, no need to do anything. Imagine you are floating on your back on water... releasing everything, because you are feeling safe and completely supported by the water. You are so relaxed that all tensions dissolve...

Gently and slowly breathe into your heart and slowly breathe out from your heart. Breathe in again and fill your body with breath, then gently exhale. Now breathe more deeply into your heart as if reaching behind the physical heart to your back and connect with your *inner* heart centre. Breathe again into your back. Feel the vastness of the universal heart –

Bring forth your fears. Let them surface. Summon them knowing this is a time for release. Let them appear and be felt. Feel your fears – whatever they maybe: financial, survival, fear for your children, fear of loss of the world as we know it, fear of rejection, of failure, of success. Give them time to surface... allow the fears to be present with all their sensations, like fluttering in your stomach or the feeling your heart is sinking. Or they wake you up in the middle of the night and it's hard to fall back to sleep. You wake in the morning feeling disconcerted, or slightly depressed. Let the fears come forth and identify them. Pause…

Breathe again deep into your heart. Feel the vastness of the universal heart and its ever-present love and compassion. It is so vast that everything and anything you or I could ever fear is unconditionally loved and accepted, absorbed as universal feelings. Breathe in your fears as you have identified and carry them to the universal heart...breathe in again and hold your breath. Pause...and drop them into the universal heart of love and transformation. Breathe out. Let them go and see them absorbed into the ocean of the heart. Feel the energy of the fears being released. Breathe in, 'letting go', and breathe out, 'letting go' for a few times. Pause…now breathe into your entire body... Imagine loving breaths filling every cell in your body. Smile from your heart to all your cells as you gently breathe throughout the body. Every cell is smiling back at you. All fear gone.

Meditation Insight(s) / Reflection

Use this page to write what came up for you in your *Letting Go of Fear into the Universal Heart Meditation.* If nothing at all arose, don't worry, insights often occur some time after meditation.

Diffusing resentments and blame

A particularly strong negative charge comes from holding resentments and blame - the type of negative energy that literally hangs around our cells, from this and other life times. Some are family-linked and carried in our DNA. A dramatic example would be an Italian family vendetta.

Here is a practice that can help diffuse this negative charge. **Think of a resentment you are still holding.** It could be an event or a relative. Stay with the feeling and the situation. Try to recall the way you felt then and be with how you feel now. **Contemplate:** "Our resentments come from a feeling of being hurt, maligned, betrayed, disrespected, ignored or taken for granted. Our hot buttons were pressed. That is our point of view. It's possible that the person inflicting the negative state upon us did so unwittingly, maybe out of their own fears, without malice in their heart, with no plan to hurt you." Try to accept such a possibility. There was no intention to hurt you. Even if a harmful intention was present, continuing to remember the grievance in your heart is hurting you. It is time to let go. **Now, imagine giving this person love and understanding** and see them receiving your love and understanding. Imagine yourself receiving their love and understanding, because there was no malice intended. Feel the negative charge dissipating, as you take several 'letting go' breaths. Even if the hurt was intended, harbouring the 'legitimate' resentment only hurts you further and saps your vital and valuable energy. Let it go also, by breathing letting go breaths.

Stop taking things personally

In relationships of every kind there can be challenges. One of our human tendencies is to take things personally and react. Our evolutionary calling is to shift away from personal reactivity and *change* the energy by remembering each other's divinity and that we are all part of the same One. In an unpleasant situation, we can pause, take note of the ego-emotional-wave and decide to shift. Smile and think of a loving remark, change the subject to something more uplifting and conciliatory or imagine sending the energy of love from your heart. It's very powerful.

Back in my corporate days I used to send love ahead of me to meetings with clients, particularly if there were difficult personalities attending. The meeting would always go smoothly. Love paved the way. (Louise Hay taught me this one!)

Opening to Grace

Grace opens up our "soul intelligence", which is beyond logic. Grace will move us from our self-absorbed and self-centered perspective to an experience of our interconnectedness and Oneness. Meditation is the means to connect us to our inner heart centre and where Grace unites us with our soul.

Transforming Mantras

Sanskrit mantras open the heart and help us to stay focussed in meditation. A mantra is a set of words or sounds charged with transformative energy, such that when we repeat them, there is a powerful cleansing of our mind and body! The sacred words are infused with 'live' energy that dissolves our negativities and opens the heart.

Natural So Hum mantra

This mantra is known as the 'heart mantra'. It is the natural sound of our breath. If we were to listen intently, we will hear: "So" and "Hum" as we breathe in and out. This mantra opens the heart, and what gives it its power, is the energy of One-ness contained within it.

"So" means "I", **"Hum"** means "that": "I am that". The in-breath and the out-breath are two aspects of breathing. We come to understand that we are actually two aspects of the same thing, like the breath. I am human and I am divine. This understanding can extend to the polarities of love and hate, despair and hope, for example. These emotions are also two aspects of the same energy. The energy in the mantra encodes our understanding and we can shift from one to another with ease. As we use the mantra, we are no longer governed by the polarities, because the mantra's power dissolves our sense of separation and the obscuration shielding the heart.

So Hum Repetition:
Say it out loud or silently to yourself
"So" on the in-breath..."Hum" on the out-breath
Feel its energy vibration

CHAPTER 5

How to Connect with Our Soul Purpose

1. Say "Yes" to life!

Tantric teachings say we find ourselves and our role by welcoming life: "Yes" to the inevitable hurdles, understanding life serves to bring us into alignment with our divine selves. There is the opportunity for growth and enlightenment in every experience. This sounds so trite or even impossible when we are in the thick of a tragic, miserable event. It's usually when we are some distance away that we can see the learning we've obtained. Our challenge is to continue to try to detect the new awareness we are receiving under all life dramas. Feel not a victim of life, but be prepared to grow through the challenges, and look for the golden nuggets inside them.

2. Listen to daily soul guidance

Connect with our inner heart centre in quiet moments in the day. When we follow intuition, our role is revealed. If we stop saying 'No' to those subtle nudges, our alignment to soul gets better! When we live in tune with our divine purpose, our daily actions feel guided from within. We surrender to the flow, resistance dissolves and we are in harmony with life. There will be difficulties, but we can tune into our soul and the bigger picture for guidance and inspiration in the heart on how to ride the waves. Be open to Love.

3. Focus on our soul gifts

Finding our soul purpose is about opening to our talents, strengths and characteristics, some of which need to be accepted. It's great to write them down, makes it easier to 'see' them. Write down even the ones we are reluctant to own. We tend to hide ourselves away, because the small ego tries to keep us limited, plus old conditioning from family and society. Excitingly, we have a part of us that was never wounded, already whole and complete. Two real life examples are JFK and Bill Clinton, who focused on being great presidents even with some ego issues! When we are accessing that healthy whole part of ourselves, we are energized and everything just flows. We feel enthused and passionate, and even a little daring!

If we focus on the gifted parts, our ego issues don't distract, and then recede. Only the things that deserve attention become energized. By stepping into our true nature, and having the courage to detach from the old fears and patterns, we make our way forward. Wherever we place our attention, whatever we think, expands. Provided we are not emotionally traumatized or in a physical crisis (which obviously requires help and attention), we can accelerate our evolution by placing our attention on the things we do really well, that turn us on and make us feel alive.

4. Own our shadows

We all have a shadow side to our nature, which has been described as sinful in Judaea Christianity. This doctrine makes us feel bad and holds us in a state of unworthiness. Also, in many Eastern traditions there is the encouragement to *purify* so that we can transcend our shadow nature. Kundalini awakening is a way purification can occur, combined with our efforts to change. The Sri Vidya Tantric tradition suggests we embrace our shadows as perfect human expressions, which doesn't mean we can't change, but change comes faster when we embrace our shadows with affection like friends and allies rather than as enemies. Only now am I able to delight in my shadow side as simply being part of who I AM - my complexity and individual nature. My shadows have taken me into the human cave so I can appreciate the human condition more fully. If we were all 'good' and not open to tasting new things, wouldn't life be boring? I AM who I AM! Enjoy!

5. Open the heart knot with meditation and mantras

There is a subtle knot of the ego holding us back from fully opening to our divinity. It is in our subtle bodies at the heart - a knot of separation from the divine. The knot is called Vishnu granthi. Vishnu is the Hindu God of Maintenance. This symbolically reflects our tendency to want to hold onto status quo, not allowing old modes of thinking and being to dissolve to create new ones. It binds the ego to doer-ship and attachment to the physical realm, attachment to compassion and to alleviation of suffering. There is nothing wrong with that; however, as we evolve, we understand that challenges and suffering are for our expansion. We learn to allow a person's soul journey to occur by stepping back and not engaging so actively in being their saviour: preventing, relieving or fixing. We become a 'compassion master' with support and love. Our egos like to 'do' and 'control', whereas unravelling the knot is surrendering to God - to the divine inside us and allowing each person to have their full experience.

6. Use the tool of the mantra

Mantras are consciousness in the form of sacred words or sounds. They have the power to transform. The mantra *Om Namah Shivaya* is very powerful and it is at the heart of Tantra. It is known as the great redeeming mantra for its power to grant *both* worldly fulfillment and spiritual realization. *OM* is the primordial sound, *Namah* is to honor with reverence; *Shivaya* means "to Shiva" or "to divine Consciousness". A simple translation would be, **'I surrender to the divine within me"** This mantra is alive with transforming energy and has been continuously chanted by enlightened Beings throughout the ages to support its energy of transformation. It mends or restores our physical and subtle bodies and opens our hearts. We can use it to aide our meditation practice, by repeating it silently on our in-breath and out-breath to quell a busy mind. Or we can say it out loud either chanting (singing) it, or by saying it in constant repetition, known as Japa. Continuous repetition through chanting or saying the mantra enhances its potency and leads to liberation. Its energy regenerates every cell, filling it with light, dissolves all negativities, misunderstandings, clears the heart; **unravels the heart knot and breaks the bondage of ego identification.** We can feel the reverberations of healing sound in every cell. We are rejuvenated and full of light. Look into the eyes of another after chanting. You will see the light in their eyes shining back at you!

I recommend several versions in the Resources Section at the back of the book, so that you can download the mantra from I-tunes and play it wherever you go.

Aligning the Ego with the Soul using a Mantra

Before meditation, offer the following prayer to open the heart knot. *"I allow the flow of life to move in its own way. I allow old models to dissolve, trusting something far greater for the collective good will be created. I allow each person the dignity of their own journey, their own experiences and opportunities for growth. No saving or pressure to be 'normal'. I accept that another's journey may be unconventional and include some deep suffering for their soul's reasons. I can be there as a benign loving support, full of light, discerning when assistance is necessary and when it is not. I trust in the process in a loving way, giving constant unconditional love. I let go of trying to control. I surrender to the divine in me, to the flow of life and I'm open to new possibilities."*

Sit quietly and relax your face and eyes. Close your eyes and place your hands on your lap or on your thighs. If sitting in a chair sink back and feel the support of the chair. Place your feet hip-width apart, firmly planted on the ground and feel roots from the soles of your feet going down into the earth. If sitting cross legged, feel the roots extending down from your sitting bones, relax your shoulders and gently elongate your spine. Take a couple of deep breaths in and deep breaths out... ...

We are going to use the Sanskrit mantra Om Namah Shivaya in this meditation. It means *"I surrender to the divine within me"* It carries the energy of transformation as it has been chanted by great beings for 1000s of years.

Bring your attention to your heart. Place your hands in prayer position and breathe into your hands your intention to enter the *inner* heart centre...

Breathe into your heart; breathe out from your heart. Relax your hands and place them on your knees or lap. Breathe into your heart again; fill your whole body with breath. Exhale gently. Breathe deeply into your heart, as if reaching behind the physical heart to your back and connect with your *inner* heart centre. Feel the vastness of the universal heart, of spacious awareness... now breathe normally.

Focus on your breathing. On the in-breath silently say, *Om Namah Shivaya* and on the out-breath say, *Om Namah Shivaya*. This mantra means *'I surrender to the divine within me"*. Say the mantra on the in-breath and on the out-breath silently for several minutes... *Om Namah Shivaya, 'I surrender to the divine within me"*. Repeating it frees you from the binds of the heart knot, the binds of the ego so you can connect directly with your soul. As you repeat the mantra you can feel its energies clearing the gateway to your soul. Pause....breathing. 2 min. Now bring your attention back into the room and when you are ready open your eyes.

YouTube: https://youtu.be/DjeFCEdOh-c?si=6Avz9fntF8cx7_5q

Meditation Insight(s) / Reflection

Use this page to write what came up for you in your *Aligning the Ego with the Soul using a Mantra*. If nothing at all arose, don't worry, insights often occur some time after meditation.

CHAPTER 6

Cultivating Our Gifts

Last chapter we covered tuning into soul guidance and aligning with our soul purpose. One particular suggestion was to focus on the things we do well rather than the ego's negative distractions. By doing so, a sense of accomplishment and satisfaction builds and we feel gratitude. Our inner reservoir of strength is filled when we are in alignment with our soul purpose. We talked about our highest soul destiny, which stems from an intention to serve humanity's spiritual evolution above our personal ego desires.

Our highest soul destiny comes from living our soul purpose, which starts with recognizing, accepting, then owning and experiencing our full range of gifts and talents! We are much bigger than we allow! Our ego carries negative limitations, full of fears and doubts, and a sense of smallness. We may have a knowing of our gifts and talents, but shy away from some that seem too grand, too much of a stretch, or we avoid others, because we fear failure. Accordingly, some have remained dormant up until now. Our *soul* destiny may actually include gifts that are in this dormant category, so we need to be alert to *all* our talents and come to own each and every one of them.

Front-Line gifts

The initial phase is recognizing our 'front-line' gifts – those that flow effortlessly to you that you do very well without trying.

Back in my time of grieving over my husband's sudden death, I was completely shattered. It was like my own death. Under his guidance from spirit, I was trying to define who I was. Even though I felt no desire for my gifts, I could see that gardening I could just do, painting I could just do and other design things I could just do. When I painted a picture, I asked my guides for help and they did. Then I said to myself, "So, I can paint" with a 'so what' attitude. Then I had to fix a wall ornament of dried pastas and beans that got weevils inside. I filled it full with beautiful crystals. I almost threw them in, with no interest at all! I was surprised when I finished. It looked really good. It seemed as though my inborn gifts just flowed, whether I was enthused or not!

While reflecting on this point, I realized that, because I wasn't able to be enthused or put my heart into those talents, I had no sense of accomplishment, no satisfaction and no gratitude, so I remained very weak and empty. I continued to have no inner reserves to draw on. I'm not blaming myself, because I was unable to summon up gratitude for anything. Now, I fully understand how important gratitude is to make us strong inside to secure our authentic selves, even when others don't get it!

Gratitude is pivotal for the activation and manifestation of our soul blueprint.

My experience of the lack of gratitude reinforced the need to practice gratitude for *all* our gifts and be mindful that there maybe a few we will take for granted, where we don't even recognize the gift factor. Becoming consciously aware of *all* our gifts, nurturing every one with gratitude, feeds our soul and shines our light. Every day notice a gift, if you can, and give thanks.

Try this exercise.

Think of what you can 'just do' without really trying; what you fully know to be true about you - your 'front-line' characteristics and gifts. They don't have to be activities, but can be: "I'm good at listening to people", "I encourage people" "I connect people with the right people", "people really trust me, particularly those..." Contemplate and write them down.

Affirm out loud, your characteristics and gifts. Feel the vibration, feel how saying them out loud energizes you. You are in your spirit!

Latent gifts.

Think of other talents you aren't as sure about that may be latent gifts, just seeds at the moment. They could be gifts you noticed, but shied away from. Even those you think are opposite to a gift: things you dread being asked to do, because you are so afraid. There may be a gift hidden inside the fear. Allow them to emerge too. For instance, I had a fear of public speaking, rooted in a stammer that developed after my father died when I was 5 yrs old. For years I even stammered my name! *However, my soul wanted me to speak* and in my career in the corporate world, initially in marketing where I didn't expect to speak publicly, I actually did. I was trained to be a presenter and eventually I became reasonably good at presentations, but still with great discomfort.

Later in my life after David died, I was wound so tightly into a ball with grief, as I was with my dad's death, again I couldn't speak. *But my soul wasn't giving up* and after a few years, I was out there speaking again, helping a friend at his workshops. On one occasion, I was visibly shaking from head to toe in clear sight of the audience, but I stayed up there speaking. Then, I was invited to MC at my meditation centre and my speaking expanded. The highest and most transforming point was being requested by my Guru to read her poem in front of a large audience at the ashram. After that experience, I now enjoy public speaking and my voice has a mellow sound that facilitates meditation in others. It took time, grace and courage for me to step into my greatest fear zone and find the gift of my voice!

Think about your latent gifts that may be hidden in phobias, or in things you avoid because of fear. **Contemplate your latent gifts** and write them down.

Affirm your latent gifts in a positive I AM statement and say them out loud to dissolve the resistance that's been built. Accept and embrace them in your heart.

It's important to accept all our gifts, remembering the ones we feel less sure about maybe the exact ones that need to be cultivated to fulfil our soul potential and enrich our life experiences. We are much <u>more</u> than we tend to think! Our soul knows our gifts. Let your soul lead your life!

Gifts from Life Experience.

Our life journeys can provide inspiration and encouragement to others. It's good to reflect on some of the challenges we have lived through and identify the valuable teachings gleaned. For example someone I know suffered terrible sexual abuse that took most of her life to heal from. At the end of her transformation she became one of the few people with whom people with deep trauma could feel trust; they became open to her healing energy. She had reached such a depth of compassion for herself and for all those involved in this deeply distressing experience that extended to humanity in general. Her wounding became her gift to help others.

Feel your Soul Meditation

Close your eyes and place your hands on your lap or on your thighs. If sitting in a chair, place your feet hip-width apart, firmly planted on the ground and feel roots from the soles of your feet going down into the earth. If sitting cross legged feel the roots extending down from your sitting bones… Relax your shoulders and gently elongate your spine. Close your eyes. Take a couple of deep breaths in and deep breaths out, release any tension...

Bring your attention to your heart. Place your hands in prayer position and breathe into your hands your intention to enter the *inner* heart centre. Hold an intention for the subtle energy of your soul to lead your meditation. Let's start with a prayer...

> *"Please guide my meditation, show me the way, and lead me to a closer connection with you my soul. Please make me aware of the gifts I bring into this life so I can express and share them for the greater good "*

Focus your attention on the breath. Breathe in and out from your naval. Then let your energy rise up and breathe in and breathe out from your heart. Be open to allow the subtle energy of your soul to lead your meditation. Breathe naturally and observe the rhythm of the breath. Notice how you are breathing... how at the end of each out-breath is a pause and then an impulsion to breathe in—and the same at the end of the in-breath, a pause then an impulsion to breathe out. Hold your breath and feel the pressure to breathe out again. ....

Then soften and shift to another perception that you are *being breathed*. Notice how the breath is being drawn in and out by the energy within your body. The *Source* of your breath is breathing you. Your Soul energy is breathing you. Feel the sensation and relax, and continue to allow yourself to be breathed... breathing time..

In the silence ask your soul to remind you of your gifts –may be talents you had as a child, things you always loved to do, or felt attracted to—. Pause .....Ask for your unique characteristics to be revealed, pause....or may be the gift of knowledge gained through your life experiences that can benefit others. Pause to receive the guidance.....

Now continue meditating and go deeper into the silence within. Let yourself rest in the field of your soul experience, so you can remember this energy again and connect with it in daily life. Pause...... 2 min

Please bring your attention back into the room and when you are ready you can open your eyes.

Video version on YouTube:
https://youtu.be/ML8K5qJTkPI?si=Mre5IABB1pLYY6xy

Meditation Insight(s) / Reflection

Use this page to write what came up for you in your *Feel your Soul Meditation.* If nothing at all arose, don't worry, insights often occur some time after meditation.

CHAPTER 7

Expand Our Capabilities: Become Our Greatest Soul Potential

We are multi-dimensional beings

Amazingly, we are multi-dimensional beings, with multiple versions of ourselves in other dimensions. We are still ourselves at the core, but they are different representations of our same soul essence.

Everything we are aware of is manifesting somewhere. I'm not good at comprehending the physics, but I have had experiences of other dimensions in meditation and in dreams, like we are all capable of experiencing. I am very interested in our multidimensional nature. As a child, I was fascinated by a book cover of a little girl reading a book. It was a design that had the picture of the little girl reading the book and within that book, the same picture of the little girl reading the book and so it went on as far as I could see, suggesting multiple dimensions. Sometimes, even as children, our soul connects us with the ultimate truth. The profound truth is no matter what dimension we find ourselves in, whether in dreams or meditation, we are always our soul and we can be the master of what happens. We can maintain serenity no matter what. I've been noticing recently that I never have horrible dreams anymore and if a dream starts heading in that direction, I can stop the reel and change things! So with a strong alignment with our soul, we can minimize the negative *emotions* in dreams and observe the symbolic message our sub-conscious is trying to give us.

What about shifting into other dimensions consciously outside of our sleep or dream state, to explore beyond our current version of reality? Well, we can with quantum jumping. **We can quantum jump into infinitesimal successful aspects of ourselves to expand our capabilities.**

There is a technique by a man called Burt Goldman. Here's his website: www.quantumjumping.com. I've paraphrased his approach below and found it a marvellous way to step outside my limited thinking, and also to energetically lift my vibration. Quantum jumping is a way of leaping out of this ego-governed energy matrix into the vastness and power of our sub-conscious mind. It is a potent way to tap into the expanded zone of awareness where ideas and inspiration flow freely. It helps us unearth skills and wisdom from the farthest corners of our mind. Quantum jumping is based on the idea that multiple universes exist, supported by physics. In these parallel universes, different versions of you also exist. There is the full range of all the "You's" that you can imagine. Some versions who made different decisions at critical points in your life, resulting in a different life. You can meet these alternative versions of yourself. Whether you choose to take it literally or metaphorically, it helps you discover your full potential. You can quantum jump to meet countless successful aspects of you. Each one of your doubles is essentially 'you' at different frequencies. You can merge with that successful energy to bring a new ability into this dimension.

To give you an idea, I decided to meet a version of me who moved through grief more quickly. I quantum jumped into her dimension to see what insight she could give me. She said, "I kept on laughing". She meant while experiencing the pain of grief, she travelled between the two polarities of grief to joy, whereas I turned off everything. I no longer wanted to engage in life. I wanted to make a point that David mattered, so I chose a very different journey. But I took her tip to heart, as I saw her in a very spacious living place and felt her glorious presence. She was being very creative, writing books and organizing lectures—she was indeed happy and successful. I can apply her approach for my advancement now: 'keep on laughing no matter what life serves."In the quantum jump, you can think of a part of you that needs help to become even bigger and better than you currently are! Do go on his web-site to explore this. www.quantumjumping.com.

Connect with your soul for advice

Think about what you need for your soul to expand, allowing whatever to come forth. It may be help with one of the latent gifts you identified earlier **Contemplate and articulate your intention to be fully open to listen to your soul's ideas to help you expand.**

The soul most often communicates through feelings or pictures or 'thought packets' rather than detailed words. It's best to connect with our soul in meditation. We can go within and ask a question, and an answer may be given then or some time later. The insight can be given in a subtle way, or for some people, in full descriptive language that's received like a 'download'. If this happens, it's good to write it down.

Merge with the Energy of Our Soul Meditation

Breathe in and out from your heart centre. Breathe deeply into your heart, as if reaching behind the physical heart to your back and connect with your inner heart centre, the seat of your soul. Suspend disbelief and be open to the possibility of having a direct access to and full merging with your soul.

Eastern philosophy talks of the universe being held in the Blue Pearl, which can be seen in meditation. The teachings say manifestation derives from the single point of the blue pearl, like a magnificent seed. Let's think of our soul as the Blue Pearl of our individual, creative potential, our brilliant seed. We are able to connect with the Blue Pearl in our hearts and with whatever our soul wants to reveal to us at this time. Picture the Blue Pearl in your heart and mentally travel towards it. Step into it and feel the presence of your soul. Feel its energy filling your body. Elongate your spine more to accommodate the energy. Feel the vibration; merge with its energy...

Spend time there, drinking in the frequency that is you, your soul. You may feel considerably bigger, like you are a great ball of energy. Settle into that sensation - the feeling of a greater you. You can connect here again and again, and carry this feeling of your greatness into everyday life...

Stay in this experience for a few minutes...

Ask your soul for a particular message that will help you manifest your soul purpose. Maybe a symbol or a *feeling*, or an understanding, or a *knowing*, or an inner certainty comes to you. Just sit and be bathed in the totality of this connection: your soul to you, your most intimate self - the one who knows everything about you, every thought you have, every word you utter -sacred or not - every step you make, every breath you take and loves you every minute, from the sublime to the anything else, which is often ridiculous! Enjoys all the ego things about you, never ceases loving the divine you, playing the game of Consciousness...

Feel the unconditional love. Rest and listen. Sense what is being offered. Now continue meditating and go deeper into the silence within.

Meditation Insight(s) / Reflection

Use this page to write what came up for you in your *Merge with the Energy of Your Soul Meditation*. If nothing at all arose, don't worry, insights often come forward some time after meditation.

CHAPTER 8

Finding Our Passion, Allow it to Unfold to Manifest Our Soul Potential

Manifestation Process

Our soul destiny unfolds by following daily guidance and slowly, and organically a new life comes to light as new doorways open. Each day involves making choices, raising the question, *"Which is the right one"?* My husband David always guided me from spirit that good choices made me *feel full*, bad choices made me *feel empty* and that's true of the companions we meet on the road. <u>Stay with whoever makes you feel full and leave those who make you feel empty.</u> No matter how wonderful they may be, they are no longer serving your soul's need for expansion. This can be a time of upheaval for friendships too, because it is so important to align with like minds.

We become the company we keep, keep good company.

Our greatest soul potential and highest destiny comes from making the shift from 'I' to 'We' consciousness, and by having the courage to offer all our gifts, free from our small ego doubts for the highest good of ourselves and everyone. We own our front-line gifts and then our dormant gifts, and for many people, it is an intimidating experience to say out loud their positive characteristics and abilities due to societal and family conditioning. For our collective evolution, it is of paramount importance that we become our authentic selves <u>no matter what anyone else around us thinks.</u>

Andrew Cohen comments on this in his book, *Evolutionary Enlightenment*, that we will encounter the collective ego inside ourselves, particularly the drive for security and familiarity. Unless we free ourselves from a stuck orientation to life, we will not evolve. He states, *"Most human beings don't live for change"*. It isn't easy to ignore cultural influences, but it is essential, if we are to fulfil our highest destiny. Getting support from like minded people helps us stay in integrity avoiding the tendency to be a little afraid to step outside the box when creating on our own. With the right support group we can keep our authenticity, and benefit from their inspiration and encouragement to materialize our self expression. Co-creation with people holding similar attitudes keeps the essence of new ideas intact and opens the possibility for enhancements to make them even better.

Cultivating and manifesting our soul purpose

Manifesting our soul purpose starts from living and being our authentic selves, which eastern philosophy describes as our *dharma* – with the principle that dharma unfolds. Consider the dharma of a tree. It requires the unfolding from a seed to reveal the tree that is inside. There had to be the right conditions for that to happen. Similarly, the *internal* conditions have to be right for us to reveal our soul purpose. Central to developing optimal inner conditions, is the *deep commitment* to evolve spiritually. Dharma flourishes when our dreams are infused with the power of our soul's intention to evolve, rather than for personal gain. When dreaming and creating from our heart, we create for the benefit of all those around and we manifest our highest potential.

Emotions drive manifestation

Our emotional state underlies manifestation. All manifestation comes from emotion and our 'unconscious' manifestation reflects the emotions, both positive and negative of where we are today. 'Less than' expectations of our ego will manifest, and our ego focus on individual success will also manifest. As we become more conscious and use visualization techniques to manifest the things we want in our life, these desires will manifest but, will still reflect our current matrix and emotional state. Our new visions will include some old negatives and the payback of karma! We are not able to manifest great wealth, if we are still holding poverty consciousness and feeling unworthy. In relationships, the chances are we will continue to manifest the same characters in different disguises until we are aware of the karmic themes unresolved inside us.

Connecting emotionally with our soul, to manifest our soul desires.

To get beyond the limitations of the small ego's emotions, we need to connect emotionally with our soul desires. By *feeling* the desires, we must cultivate our ability to visualize and act 'as if' we are walking the walk of our soul. Moving into this connection is assisted by:

Forming a new intention: Wholeheartedly choose to step into alignment with our soul purpose as if it is the only thing that matters. Make it the primary intention of this lifetime to manifest our soul potential. Our intention is very broad rather than desiring something specific. It is very open and daring, it's saying something like, "My intention is, **I AM willing to reveal my soul, I feel and manifest my soul potential, I AM flourishing as I AM my soul, I AM Consciousness.**"

Our emotional connection can shift when we assume a new identification: Manifesting our soul purpose, requires shifting our inner state to a full consciousness of being divine. Acknowledge we are no longer a human being having a spiritual experience, but a divine being experiencing a human body. We are Consciousness, we are Infinite. All our soul wants to do is expand. Its essence is the impulse to grow and be fully open to the energy of Consciousness and the potential of this life.

Shifting out of negative emotions, forming a new attitude: Sometimes we will waver on the journey when obstacles come in the way of our greatest soul potential. They arise because they need new understanding. They are not blocks as such, but rather they are challenges carrying transformational energy that can turn into openings for spiritual expansion. Our new attitude becomes, **"We are perfect just as we are."** Drop hesitations! Say, "Yes" to life! Everything is good!

Connecting with our soul emotions: We manifest our soul desires by tapping into our soul emotions and then we act 'as if' we walk the talk of our soul. We can bond with our soul emotions by sensing our soul's energy and talking to it. We may want to quantum jump to meet our soul for clarification on issues as they come up. Feel what it's like to live as our essence. Sense our soul as a living energy that we can connect or talk with whenever we choose and will fill us with enthusiasm! As we connect, our energies align and there is a vibrational shift. We spend more time feeling positive and excited by life.

Merge with Soul Emotions and Desires Meditation

This meditation helps you to feel and merge with the emotions of your soul desire.

Sit quietly where you can relax without any disturbance. Close your eyes and place your hands on your lap. If sitting in a chair, place your feet hip-width apart, firmly planted on the ground and feel roots from the soles of your feet going down into the earth. If sitting cross legged, feel the roots extending down from your sitting bones...

Breathe in and breathe out deeply. Allow your spine to elongate on the exhale. Breathe in and breathe out. With your chin parallel to the floor, let your shoulders and your neck relax...

Breathe in and out from your heart centre. Breathe deeply into your heart again as if reaching behind the physical heart to your back and connect with your inner heart centre, the seat of your soul...

Allow yourself time to feel and hear the rhythm of your breath as it goes in and out...

Open to the possibility of a direct merging with your soul to experience the emotions of your soul's desire...

Your soul has a flame like a blue light in your heart. Imagine the light and mentally travel towards the blue light. Feel the presence of your soul in front of you... its loving energy filling your body. Elongate your spine more to accommodate this energy. Feel the vibration. Merge with its tender, warm, and caring energy...

Ask to feel the emotions it experiences, the emotions behind its desires. Spend some time with your soul, communing together; allow the emotions to fill you.—*Love, Compassion, Enthusiasm, Excitement, Happiness, Anticipation, Joy...*Allow time to feel each emotion. Drink in the emotions that are the real you, as you are your soul. Settle into that sensation, that feeling of the greater you, the joyous you, the enthusiastic you...

You can connect to your soul emotions again and again and carry the feeling of your greatness into everyday life. Stay in this experience for a few minutes.

Meditation Insight(s) / Reflection

Use this page to write what came up for you in your *Merge with Soul Emotions and Desires Meditation.* If nothing at all arose, don't worry, insights often occur some time after meditation.

CHAPTER 9

Living Our Soul Purpose and Sharing Our Blessings

An Attitude of Gratitude activates our soul blueprint

Our soul purpose is encoded in our soul's blueprint at birth. *Activating* and *manifesting* our soul blueprint requires the energy of gratitude for all that happens in life: the good and the bad plus the courage to embrace the unknown.

The feelings of accomplishment and satisfaction, derived from doing things well, make us strong inside and fill us up with the energy of *gratitude*. We feel aligned with our soul. Our reservoir of goodness builds and we can muster up more *courage* to pursue ideas that stretch us. When we choose to be in alignment with our soul blueprint, we ignore ego gyrations, we sense the evolutionary impulse of Consciousness. We are fully connected to our hearts and listen to the daily directions from our soul. It takes commitment and courage and the dare to embrace the unknown. We are entering new ways of being! Gratitude is the gateway to the new horizons and the revelation of our soul purpose.

In my own life, sometimes I become emotionally involved over what's *not* happening, wishing for something to be different, a person to be different, and these sorts of subjects can really become very absorbing for the mind, even when they are very negative! I was having one of those almost addictive thoughts when I picked up a book about gratitude. As I began to read, I newly appreciated the power of gratitude. It felt like a shower of love dissolving my negative discontent. Remembering to review each day with gratitude is a powerful practice that would be great for us all in our endeavors to live our soul purpose.

Soul purpose manifestation: Takes its own sweet time, going with the daily flow of guidance. It is ready to materialize when the conditions are right. No need to force the process, so drop expectations. It's best to welcome each day and say, "Yes" to life! We assume the *feeling and emotional state* of being our soul and keep connecting and feeling that joyous emotion and expanded energy. We choose not to listen to our small ego self and its stuff. We take actions that our soul guides us to take. Start new habits—like affirming every morning to offer our day to our soul: **"I offer myself in service to my soul, to life. I am open to all the grace and miracles coming my way today".**

When challenges arise, think, how would my soul handle this? Listen to our heart, form an intention/an attitude—act—let go and allow the soul to manifest. It will be better than our expectations. Once living our soul purpose we honour our true nature in everything we do, treat ourselves, our body and everyone we meet with love and respect. Bring the sacred into everyday life, giving gratitude at every interval and smile at everyone!

Let's close this conversation with a meditation of thanks and send blessings out into the world, fully conscious of how these prayers and intentions have a powerful effect on everyone.

Gratitude and Blessings to the World Gratitude Meditation

Sit quietly, close your eyes and place your hands on your lap. If sitting on a chair place your feet hip width apart firmly planted on the ground and feel roots from your feet going down into the earth. If sitting cross legged feel roots extending down from your sitting bones.

Breathe in and breathe out deeply and allow your spine to extend on the exhale. Breathe in and breathe out. With your chin parallel to the floor let your shoulders drop and relax.

Focus breathing into your heart and mentally say, "My life is filled with blessings. **I AM** very grateful."

Think of something or someone you feel is a blessing in your life. Imagine the situation and feel gratitude swelling in your heart, filling your whole energy field and flowing out from you into the world...

Think of someone you'd like to send blessings to and send them from your heart, feelings of love, and blessings of joy, self-fulfillment and smile. Now send the blessings out into the world, blessings of good health, material abundance and love, blessings of joy and self-fulfilment...

Imagine blessings sprinkling on everyone, from your home town to your country to the places in the world that are in strife at this point in time. Imagine any place or person your heart feels love and compassion for.

Send them blessings...

Then feel the blessings showering down on you and filling your heart, blessings of abundance, good health, inner peace and calm, and a sense of knowing what to do and when. No stress no fears. Silently say in your heart, "I AM Consciousness. I send these powerful blessings to humanity and contribute to the evolutionary shift. May everyone be treated with love and respect."

Stay for a moment or two in this blissful energy.

Video version on YouTube:
https://youtu.be/l0EUM22ag7o?si=rKXM6AlEwE8C2yb

Meditation Insight(s) / Reflection

Use this page to write what came up for you in your *Gratitude and Blessings to the World Gratitude Meditation.* If nothing at all arose, don't worry, in time it will.

RESOURCES

Books

Play of Consciousness	Swami Muktananda
Journey of Souls	Michael Newton
Evolutionary Enlightenment	Andrew Cohen
The Heart of Meditation	SallyKempton/ Swami Durgananda
Meditation for the Love of It	SallyKempton/ Swami Durgananda
Tantra, the Path of Ecstasy	George Feuerstein
Auspicious Wisdom	Douglas Renfrew Brooks
Meditate, Happiness Lies Within You	Swami Muktananda
Tantra Illuminated	Christopher D. Wallis

-----Most are available at Amazon.com-----

CD's DVD's

Om Namah Shivaya (SiddhaYoga Meditation)	Gurumayi Chidvilasananda
So Hum Mantra	YouTube 4JnA6k9Q1dM
Tamboura	J.A. Jance
Music for deep Meditation, Tamboura	Vidura Barrios
Invocation of Grace	Ty Burhoe & friends

Om Namah Shivaya	Sacred Chants of Shiva, The art of living
Om Namah Shivaya	Santa Fe Satsang, Amma Centre
The Eternal OM	Valley of the Sun
Crystal bowl Healing	Steven Halpern
Awakened Heart Meditation	Sally Kempton
Heart-Centred Meditations	Hilary Bowring
	YouTube channel
	divinealign@hotmail.com

Web-sites

Sally Kempton	www.sallykempton.com
Burt Goldman Various Lectures	www.quantumjumping.com
Heart Math institute	www.heartmath.org.
World Puja	www.worldpuja.org
Hilary Bowring	www.divinealign.com

ABOUT THE AUTHOR

 **Hilary Bowring** is the owner at **Divine Align**, (www.divinealign.com) where she offers transformative healing and spiritual coaching to individuals and teaches workshops on Meditation, Sound Healing and Eastern Philosophy. Hilary has been meditating for over 25 years and fully knows its transformative power. This new orientation to the healing arts followed a lengthy career in advertising and marketing that ended after her husband's sudden death.

"During my long dark night of the soul, after my husband's sudden death, meditation came to me as my only solace and transformer...Since then my soul purpose has been to help people meditate and feel the benefits. Having been in the stress filled world of marketing and advertising I know spending a lot of time sitting in the lotus position isn't practical! I discovered in my own exploration that 5 min each day can make a difference—a short daily practice can bring inner steadiness and calm detachment-no matter what life serves. Meditation has a mysterious transforming quality that builds on a daily basis. The impact of sudden death brought changes to my consciousness and an understanding that life is about soul journeys for spiritual evolution. My passion for living was re-ignited studying tantric philosophy, which is about self-realization in the body.

I love to write, and am an author in another book "The Thought that changed my Life" where 52 authors share moments that changed their life forever. Also a regular contributor to a global online journal "Narrative Paths Journal" and a magazine in Glastonbury England, IAMGlastonbury. I'm mostly able to see the funny side of everything! My heart's desire is to help others flourish in their lives."

**Hilary Bowring. Meditation Teacher. Soul Coach,
Energy/Sound Healer; Hypnotherapy.
Born in England, lives in Canada. Available everywhere virtually!**

- **Staying in Touch**

  If you would like to receive news of workshops and events, please join my mailing list at <u>divinealign@hotmail.com</u>. I offer individual counselling and coaching sessions in person, or on Zoom. Feel free to e-mail me for more details.

- **Videos of many of my Heart centred Meditations are available on YouTube.**

  From *Find Your Soul* and a Higher Love series. New Meditations are always being added.

I hope there is a resonance in my voice that draws you inwards to a deeper experience.

Printed in the USA
CPSIA information can be obtained
at www.ICGtesting.com
LVHW080811311023
762205LV00003B/221